Muse's Odyssey

Shruti De

BookLeaf Publishing

India | USA | UK

Presentation by *BookLeaf Publishing*

Web: www.bookleafpub.com

E-mail: info@bookleafpub.com

ISBN: 9789363319738

First edition 2024

To Jyatha, whose spirit shines brightly at the 75th,

And to all whose love illuminates my journey to eternity as my brother, 'Saswata's name echoes

ACKNOWLEDGEMENT

Writing a collection of poems has been a journey of introspection, creativity, and emotional depth. Along this path, I have been fortunate to receive support, encouragement, and guidance from many remarkable individuals whom I deeply appreciate.

First and foremost, I am grateful to my family for their unwavering support and understanding throughout this endeavor. Their love has been my anchor, allowing me the freedom to explore and express myself through poetry.

To my friends, whose companionship and conversations have sparked inspiration and shaped my perspective, thank you for your camaraderie and laughter, which have infused these poems with joy and warmth.

I extend my heartfelt thanks to my mentors and teachers whose wisdom and encouragement have nurtured my growth as a poet. Your guidance has been invaluable in refining my craft and exploring new horizons in poetic expression.

Special gratitude goes to Bookleaf Publishing for believing in my work and making my dream of sharing these poems with the world come true. Your dedication and support have been instrumental in bringing this project to fruition. Lastly, I thank the readers who embark on this poetic journey with me. Your presence gives meaning to these words, and I hope that my poems resonate with you in unexpected and meaningful ways.

Thank you all for being part of this odyssey of poetry and emotion.

Warm regards,

Shruti De

PREFACE

In the quiet corners of my heart and amidst the cadence of life's melodies, I found solace in the art of poetry. It began in the days of my youth, when words first danced upon the page, penned with a soul eager to express. At the tender age of eleven, I embarked on a journey of words, guided by the profound inspiration from my mother, Smt. Saswati De's poetry, and the gentle encouragement of two beloved souls: my Jyatha, Sri Swapan Dey and my Bengali teacher, Smt. Jayeeta Mitra. They were not just readers of my early verses; they were the pillars of understanding, parsing through my phrasings and sentences with a keen eye that only love, and wisdom can nurture.

My uncle, Jyatha, held a special place in my heart—a place that remains, though he has departed from this physical realm. My mother Smt. Saswati De, my father Sri Subir De, and Jyatha's love for the language and the arts resonated deeply within me, shaping my early perceptions and kindling a passion that would endure. Alongside him, Jayeeta Di, my teacher, bestowed upon me not only knowledge but also a profound appreciation for the power of words to convey emotions that transcend language itself.

Raised in a household where Bengali and English harmonized effortlessly, I discovered that the language of expression knows no boundaries. While my mother tongue, Bengali, holds a sacred place in my heart, English became another canvas upon which I could paint my emotions and thoughts. Like the strings of my sarod or Mohanveena, each language became an instrument through which I could weave tales of joy, sorrow, and introspection.

As an introvert, I found refuge in writing—where the pen could speak volumes that my voice sometimes struggled to articulate. Poetry became my sanctuary, especially in moments of loss and emotional turmoil. After the untimely departures of both Jyatha and Jayeeta Di, writing became not just a means of expression but a lifeline—a way to navigate the depths of grief and find solace in the beauty of memories woven into verses.

Yet, amidst the ebb and flow of life, there were times when I hesitated to share my poetry, fearing that the absence of my cherished readers would leave my words adrift. It was my brother, a literature enthusiast and author himself, who reignited the flame of sharing.

Now, as I stand on the threshold of publishing my first collection, I am humbled and grateful for this journey. These poems, each a testament to love, loss, resilience, and the myriad emotions that color our existence are more than mere words on a page. They are fragments of my soul—offered with gratitude to those who have shaped me, supported me, and loved me unconditionally.

Within these verses:

'Camaraderie' celebrates the bonds of friendship and unity amidst life's challenges. *'The Guiding Light'* honors the memory of Jyatha, imparting cultural wisdom and love. *'Revenge'* explores the ecological impact of climate change and humanity's role. *'Rebel'* challenges societal norms and encourages individuality and courage. *'Immortal Breeze'* reflects on personal grief and finding strength through memories. *"Muse's Odyssey"* explores creativity, inspiration, and the artist's journey of self-discovery. *'Rageshree and...'* celebrates the enduring power of music to transcend time and connect souls. *'Quantum Melody'* delves into

introspection, identity, and the search for inner peace. *'By the Arabian Sea'* contemplates the passage of time, memories, and the essence of existence.

This collection is a tribute—to my Jyatha, whose spirit continues to inspire, to my teacher Jayeeta Di, whose wisdom echoes in every line, and to all those who have touched my life with their kindness and belief in my words. It is with profound gratitude that I present this book, a culmination of emotions, experiences, and the enduring power of language to connect us all.

With heartfelt thanks to the Almighty, my parents, my dear brothers & Jyatha, my Guruji and all who have journeyed with me, I invite you to explore these poems—a journey that has been both deeply personal and universally human.

Thank you.

Shruti De

TABLE OF CONTENTS

The Storyteller

After the headlights dim & bells ring,
After the door opens & he enters,
After my eager face lights up,
The house becomes luminous.

Trees sing, the night sky brightens,
Energized, I dart around,
Finding my own sacred space.
He unveils the Vedas, Ramayana, and
Mahabharata,
Souls purified under the starry embrace.

The Guiding Light

He lay unresponsive, a smile on his face,
A peaceful departure, a gentle embrace.
On the first floor, he used to roam,
But the terrace garden was his true home.

With jasmine, petunia, dahlia in bloom,
Chrysanthemums brightened his room.
Watering them at dawn and dusk,
A routine he cherished, a gardener's trust.

Around his house, a garden thrived,
Trees, flowers, veggies, alive.
Insects and birds, his daily guests,
Joined him for morning tea and evening rests.

A gathering with Ramkeli, Lalit,
Durga and Puriya Dhanashree, spirits lit.
Jasmine at night in a decorative pot,
Sweet, sagacious nights, storytelling a lot.

Questions of Arjuna and Draupadi's plight,
Filled the child's mind, a curious light.
Why was a woman so disrespected,
Yet her power never fully detected?

He answered with elegance, calm and wise,
Humanity as religion in her eyes.
Her sky grew wider, her mind a kingdom,
Freedom of speech, ideals, and wisdom.

From quantum worlds to cosmic tales,
Schrödinger's cat to nebula sails.
Stars' birth and death, a child's delight,
Physics and nature, her guiding light.

"Study Physics, nature's own lore,
Discover the universe, and seek more."
He instilled a love, bold and sublime,
Difficult yet peaceful, transcending time.

Days passed, they both grew,
She a lady, and Jyatha renewed.
The day came too soon, he became a star,
Her existence shaken, left with a scar.

Unspoken words, unsung songs,
Daily discussions, now gone.
Numb with grief, yet strong in will,
She vows to fulfill his dreams still.

In wisdom, creation, and music alive,
She keeps him with her, his spirit thrives.

Kaleidoscope

On a sun-kissed Spring morning's rise,
Zeal paints the skies, our hearts aglow,
To Thacher Park we journey, wide and free,
Where vibrant horizons beckon, dancing with
glee.

Among ancient trees, hands on the wheel,
Laughter dances, voices reel,
Adventures whisper, ever near,
In nature's embrace, we find joy sincere.

You smile, you shout,
You run, you sprout,
Beneath cool canopies we retreat,
Shielded from the sun's intense heat.

Summiting history's lofty peak,
Jovial bonds, stories we seek,
Walking miles, mountains vast and grand,
Nature's beauty, hearts understand.

You climb, the breeze, a gentle tease,
Your smile, a moment seized,
Brightening my day with its grace,
In nature's embrace, a familiar place.

We witness the waterfall's symphony grand,
Its power echoes, hearts expand,
Capturing memories, bold and clear,
In shared moments, no trace of fear.

Home we return, love and memories in tow,
With greenery's peace, laughter's glow,
Singing life's song, sweet and bright,
Our journey's wisdom, hearts alight.

In your soul, untamed and true,
Every step, a journey anew,
Not confined, but free to roam,
In life's kaleidoscope, our home.

Camaraderie

That beautiful evening, you and me,
Over a pair of Fudge Sundaes,
We heard our melancholic solitude
Reverberate through the acoustics.
We fell for a millennia!

Your ravishing, euphonic voice,
My sumptuous notes on strings,
Following your compassionate pronouncements,
The immortal camaraderie in harmony sings.

Again and again I go back to the day

Again and again, I go back to the day
You came in.
Your inquisitive mind asked
Innumerable questions.
Irritation surpassed, prevailing over time,
At the end, I found in you a child of nine.

Again and again, I go back to the day
You came in.
We invigorated, thrilled, tried finding
A solace.
Emotions overwhelmed, desires fulfilled,
I found astounding love, care, and innocence.

Again and again, I go back to the day
You came in.
I lose, I find, I cry, I smile,
Peering through the window of time.
Though I lost your physical abode,
I knowYou are mine.

Revenge

Wandering meadows, lands, and woods,
It leads me to the griefs of the hoods.
The sea, once pristine, now oily,
Ecology harmed, lives spoiled wholly.

Rising levels, unbound in plight,
Climate strikes back with all its might.
No more respite, no time to doze,
For it knows,
"Strife beats the silence of woes."

Rebel

Knowing more and more about less and less,
One sees mostly haze and mirage.
The rebellious sky is torn apart,
Global warming evident in every part.
Fulminant diseases take their forms,
To the ultimate, out of the norms.
The kingdoms of all sentient creatures
Silently calling out!

No! The supreme intelligence deafens,
Outmaneuvering around,
Treacherous acts on the greenery,
Even on the waterbodies found.
On everything that's natural,
Extinction of lives, turning them to relics.
Now the tide begins to shift!

Thousand years of disastrous carbon footprints
Have become bold dissenters.
The new rebel is formed
Against the callous care of artificial livelihood.
The summer grows hotter, the winter so,
The rain brings droughts in a row.

Arise and awake, it's time to restore,
Emerge from old ways, let the spirit soar!
Look around at what you've made and lost,
Strive for renewal, no matter the cost!

The Nocturnal Crisis

A night of painstaking breaths,
Heaven weeps in mourning cries,
Clouds hang low, burdened and bereft,
Winter's grip, deadly under snowy skies.

Terrifying loneliness pervades,
As all that was vibrant now dies.
I shiver, a sigh escapes,
Pages yellowed, shattered pathways lie.

Within, the rose stains with blood,
Surroundings deadly, a gasp of despair,
Red turns terrible at the sight,
I shiver, weighed by this night's dark flair.

Pitiful sorrow surrounds,
Cuts through flesh, skin, and bone,
A child's cry trembles the ground,
I shiver, echoing a night so alone.

The darkest night, relentless in its stride,
Where despair and shadows collide.

Childhood

It's all about the quintessential past,
In glee, spending time in heavy spree.
The 6 o'clock school bus waiting in front,
The kid rising from bed.
Mom chases behind,
Feeding her as much as she could,
With a cute tiffin box in hand.

Her bag is ready to go, she quickly dons her
uniform,
In the zeal of doing classes.
Studying is her choice,
Along with all sorts of artistic activities,
A cherished dream she lives.

She runs, Mom runs behind.
She gets to the bus, Mom returns with peace in
her mind.

She reaches school, meets her friends,
Speaks about homework and Feluda.
The detective stories win her mind.
She lives and relives, dreams and redreams,
Setting in the adventures of Feluda,
Pradosh Chandra Mitra, PCM.
The prayer bell rings.

She is a leader with plenty of responsibilities.
She enters the classroom, requests everyone
To assemble,
Asking them to follow her.
She steps towards the huge, historic prayer room
of her school.
The second bell rings, and they start singing in
chorus:
"Lead me from the unreal to the real,
Lead me from darkness to light,
Lead me from death to immortality.
May peace be, may peace be, may peace be."

A Mother - The World

Afternoons were hers, mornings too,
Nights where she finds brief rest.
Her lullabies softly guide children to sleep.

She cooks,
She imparts music, art, reading, and compassion,
She loves unconditionally,
Regardless of acquaintance.
She embraces everyone with her heart,
The most honest soul I've ever known.
Her songs summon angels
To Heaven's doorstep.
Her discretion and grace are boundless,
Sacrifices for her dear ones, made without a
sound.
She, the cornerstone of existence,
Life's essence personified.
She is 'Mom'.

Backbone

From Ahiri's dawn to Kaushiki's dusk,
The morning breeze renews the child,
With all its zest and fervent trust,
Embracing life's melody, serene and wild.

Under her father's tender gaze,
She is nurtured, molded, and refined,
With boundless care, passion ablaze,
A symphony within her mind.

Surreal music flows through her veins,
As her father practices by her side,
Cradling her, as soft as summer rains,
In his lap, where love and music reside.

Thus, she blossomed, pure and true,
A worshipper of melodic grace,
In every note, her spirit grew,
Reflecting her father's loving embrace.

The Lidder

Verdant green prairies stretch,
The cradle of Lidder's flow,
Its waters pristine,
Gushing over riverbed stones,
A source of solace,
For pilgrims' souls.

A log cabin nestles beside its dear flow,
Radiating harmonious glow.
Majestic mountains stand sentinel,
Protecting Lidder, meadows, and vines,
The sky mirrors its azure flow,
Echoing Bahar in tranquil rhythm.

A peasant guides her sheep along,
Serenity inspires a poet's song,
Verse flowing like the river's course,
A deluge of imagery,
Elysian to eye and ear.

Rageshree and…

The ambiguities linger, silently debate,
Whether I love him or merely await fate's
dictate.
My heart rejoices in his presence near,
Words exchanged mold courage from within.

He enters with sincere care,
Apathy and mundane concerns disperse, rare.
My heart swells with Rageshree's embrace,
Melodic beauty entwines, leaving no space.

Microtones form, forging paths anew,
Determination rises, steadfast and true.
Love within struggles to believe,
Haunted by memories that make it grieve.

Together we sang, tears intertwined,
Dreams of a paradise, our minds combined.

Parting pains deeply,
Inside, a deluge of hurt rains steadily.
Yet, I hold on to memories of peace,
Cherishing moments, longing for release.

I do not know if this is love's true test,
My honesty reveals my heart's unrest.
I blush, I weep, I soar,
In love with him, forever more.

Immortal Breeze

Beside the lake, deep below,
An island stands,
Home to migrating birds.
The trees, now leafless,
Still offer shelter.

Their chirping weaves an evening melody,
With a reluctant, ethereal voice of togetherness.
Twilight shadows fall on wandering faces,
'Jamuna ki teer' whispers in the ears,
Bhairavi sets the tune for the day's end.

Meandering along the trails,
Through trees and bushes,
The loquacious migrating birds,
The essence of beholding treasure,
Brings you back to the present.

My eyes cannot see you,
But my heart echoes yours...

Silent Notes

A blocked door, the windows shut
Sunrays are restricted to enter..
The path inside goes beyond
Through the unwoven woods,
Greenery and meadows!

The nascent silence,
Strikes loud,
Just like a string strums unwittingly
And
And a somber melody harmonizes disparity!

Endlessly

Going over again and again
Through the lines of blue,
Seems crossing an unbridgeable chasm
Breathlessness surrounds.

The darkest night ever
She waits for a bang on the door;
Droplets of mystic Rain,
Sings a melancholic Megh Malhar
It never ends...!

By the Arabian Sea

The night by the Arabian Sea,
Quiet, melodious, and starry,
Together we sat by the shore,
My pensive, lonely eyes
Met his dreamy, tender breaths.
You heal past scars, gently filling them with
love,
The night by the Arabian Sea.

The sea's salty fragrance, so familiar,
As my tears flow, unbounded.
You sing notes that touch the soul,
My face rests on your shoulder,
The night by the Arabian Sea.

Your voice, a melodious whisper,
Permeates deep within me,
My lips murmur your name,
Tears unstoppable,
Knowing the night is not infinite.
Peaceful nights return, again and again,
Your silence speaks volumes,
The night by the Arabian Sea.

You hold my hand, calm yet trusting,
We sit still, side by side,
Gazing at the deep Arabian Sea and starry sky,
We are timeless,
The night by the Arabian Sea.

Night & Day, Dusk and Dawn

A soul stirs up a thought,
a part of it left behind,
far away, long away,
a vacuum takes its place.

The other part remains,
in trance and trauma,
the past prevails.

Leaves of the trees bow in obeisance,
the stream flows unbound,
Gaud Sarang in the air.

Love and restlessness cuddle close,
disguised in harmony.

Epitaph

Erected on the ground,
a stone of remembrance found:
Father Charles Keeler, passed in 1916,
Mother Evelina Laning, departed in 1903,
and their son, Edward, in 1900.

Their thirty-year-old son, lost to war,
parents proud yet sorrowful for sure.
Their hearts bereft of affection and love,
losing their only child, high above,
memories painfully clear.

Mother passes three years later,
seclusion consumes the father,
he withdraws from the world's chatter,
it takes thirteen more years...

Then they reunite,
a family forever in the light,
together they rest,
never to part in their blessed nest.

Oh Vincent!

Intricacies of his opus
Mesmerize the mind
As one gazes upon his
Starry night.

The communion with him
Was deeply personal,
I began to see him
As my soul's echo.

The exquisite brushstrokes whisper emotions
Of radiant sunflowers and windswept sails.
They unveil a celestial beauty
In hues of azure and gilded.
Each stroke a heartbeat, each hue a sigh,
A glimpse of the universe through your
perceptive eye.

Fields of wheat and skies ablaze,
Capture your ardor, your everlasting flame.
In quiet chambers with walls of ivory,
You painted dreams, wrestled with the night.

In anguish, an uncanny fondness,
I find solace in your life and art.

A troubled heart akin to mine,
In every masterpiece, you impart,
A fragment of yourself, forever captured
In the celestial muse of thought.

Your legacy, Vincent, a beacon bright,
Guides dreamers and seekers alike,
In your turmoil, a tranquil refuge,
In your passion, an eternal spark,
Forever intertwined with the stars and the
secrets,
In the silent sanctuary of art.

Quantum Melody

When she strikes the strings of her
Afghani Rabab with a plectrum,
Bageshree opens the door.
Fragrant sandalwood, the smell of old books,
It's the entrance to the bibliophile's place,
Condensation to sophistication.

Notes linger, her imagination too,
The classical approach to the quantum sphere,
Effects sublime to the beauty of the beholder.
It stares, speaks, sings through M P D M g,
Alpha, beta, gamma, delta, kappa, theta, zeta,
sigma,
All become her connoisseurs.

The glass door vibrates as if the notes pervade,
Shaking its core.
The wave passes by, treasuring its particle
duality,
The soothingness of the raag reverberates As a
calming melody,
Superconducting emotions within.

She is in meditation,
Gravitational agitation on her fingerboard,
Creating a symphony of the soul…!